Burdened

When We Pray We ENTERcede

I0555024

Timbacka Vangure

REJOICE
Essential Publishing

I

Timbacka Vangure/Rejoice Essential Publishing

PO BOX 512

Effingham, SC 29541

www.republishing.org

Unless otherwise indicated, scripture is taken from the King James Version.

Burdened/Timbacka Vangure

www.bearingfruitca.com

Scripture taken from the New King James Version®. Copyright © 1982 by Thomas Nelson. Used by permission. All rights reserved.

ISBN-13: 978-1-956775-67-9

Table of Contents

Introduction

Before going to the cross, Jesus found His disciples repeatedly sleeping and asked them a simple but thought-provoking question. He said, "Are you STILL sleeping and resting and the hour has come when the Son of man will be taken and delivered into the hands of sinners." In this instance, it seemed as though Jesus lacked support during His time of distress. During a very important transition, I found myself needing prayer and later realized it needed to come from me. Prayer was the only answer I had to my constant discontent, confusion, and frustration. Arming myself with the incomparable tool of prayer got me through. Here I have compiled a list of prayers to help you along the journey. Whether you are praying for yourself or someone else, just as Jesus says, "The hour has come. "It is time to pray. Allow these prayers to guide and assist you into greater.

1

God's Will

Father, as you commanded the winds and waves to be settled, so shall there be a settling concerning me. As I seek the thoughts You have concerning me, so shall I seek that which is above. I will taste and see the goodness of You Lord. Lord, help me not to overthink or under think the things You have, but stay the course. As I lean not to my own understanding, allow stability, strength, and courage to replace doubt, fear, and double-mindedness in Jesus' name.

Divine Help

I declare no more pot holes and pitfalls of disappointment on the road of my life. I declare no more rocky travel and confusing directions on my way to destiny. As I pursue, destiny is moving towards me. Opposition and resistance are dismantled by clarity and direction in the name of Jesus. Victory is within my reach and help is extended to me. No weapon formed against me shall prosper. Lord, guide me to the doors you opened for me and strengthen me to walk through boldly. Let my heart not be troubled when You have pointed out the directions or the connections I shall pursue in Jesus' name.

What If's

Lord, I now take authority over ALL what-ifs. What-ifs intending to cause false concerns, false imaginations, fear, over thinking, stagnation, anxiety, distraction, and doubt. I will not allow good seed sown to be choked by the thoughts and worries of what ifs. Instead, I know that You have plans set aside to prosper me and to give me hope and a future in Jesus' name.

Increase

Lord, as I cast out my net in faith, let there be increase.

Let there be increase as I let out my net for more.

Let there be increase as I let out my net for direction.

Let there be increase as I let out my net for abundance.

Let there be increase as I let out my net for new connections and relationships.

Let there be increase as I let out my net for better finances and income.

Let there be increase as I let out my net for _____
Fill in the blank.

Progress

Father, as I seek first the kingdom, all things are coming together.

As I seek first the kingdom, all things are being added

As I seek first the kingdom, I am whole.

As I seek first the kingdom, I am victorious.

As I seek first the kingdom, my health is well.

As I seek first the kingdom, my mind is settled.

As I seek first the kingdom, my heart is healthy.

As I seek first the kingdom, my thoughts are sound.

As I seek first the kingdom, my faith is steadfast.

Wisdom

Father, as every good gift comes from You and Your constant-infinite ability, let Your wisdom prosper me. Let Your wisdom set me on track. Let Your wisdom guide me. Let Your wisdom carry me. Let Your wisdom govern me. Let Your wisdom pursue me. Let Your wisdom befriend me. Let Your wisdom cover me in Jesus' name.

In The Wait

Lord, allow me to receive favor in the wait.
Lord, allow me to receive blessings in the wait.
Lord, allow me to gain ground in the wait.
Lord, allow me to produce in the wait.
Lord, allow me joy in the wait.
Lord, allow me help in the wait.
Lord, allow no frustrated in the wait.
Lord, allow no confusion in the wait.
Lord, allow me not to be stuck in the wait.
Lord, allow me not to be wayward in the wait.
Lord, allow me not to be ashamed in the wait.
Lord, allow me clarity in the wait.
Lord, allow me victory in the wait.
Lord, allow me assurance in the wait.
Lord, allow me protection in the wait.
Lord, allow me strength in the wait.

8

Lord, allow me direction in the wait.
Lord, allow me abundance in the wait.
Lord, let not the wait weigh me down.

Relief

Father, as you allow all who are heavy burdens to come unto you, so shall there be a release of relief.

Let there be relief in situations of discontent.

Let there be relief in times of financial difficulties.

Let there be relief in battles of the mind.

Let there be relief in times of uncertainty.

Let there be relief in times of disbelief.

Let there be relief in the times of wait.

Let there be relief.

Continuing After God's Instructions

Father, as You have settled the matter and provided instructions, I declare I will not be weighed down with false sentiment or false emotionalism. I will move in truth and be in joy and expectancy, being led, guided, and strengthened by Your Holy Spirit. I will be present in what You are doing and continue to persevere. I declare Your strength and wisdom for the journey in Jesus' name.

Mind and Sight

Struggle

Father, as I renew my mind daily, I am strengthened by the authority You have given me to tread over scorpions. That which desires to blind the sight of my mind has no ability. Father, continue to connect dots and smother thoughts not in alignment with the vision You have for me. Negative thoughts, cycles, mind battles, and distractions have no authority in Jesus' name.

Renewed

God, allow a new and fresh wind to take precedence. Let it usher in wholeness, favor, clarity, protection, joy, and all things good. Allow no weapon formed to prosper as this new wind commands its place. Allow all witchcraft and demonic presence to be removed with its current. And let there be a rest and reset in Jesus' name.

Strength

Father, give me the courage to do, say, go, and be exactly what you intend. Allow love, power, and a sound mind to accompany me. Let provision, favor, protection, alignment, clarity, grace, and mercy be before me on the journey. Direct me to the right doors and allow favor and opportunity to greet me at the entrance. Lord, give me the ability and courage to knock, seek, and find all in Jesus' name.

Wicked Plots

Father, let every word concerning me not from You bear no fruit. As the wicked plant evil words towards me and all connected to me let their words fall, be trampled, and devoured by the fowls of the air. Words of no merit shall lack depth and other negative words shall chock on themselves. Father break the wings of negative assignments sent and let them return with no success in Jesus' name.

Disappointment

Father, as disappointment desires to overtake me, cut off both its head and tail. For I am above and not beneath.

Let evil assignments, negative intent towards me, and strategic and planned disappointments and failure be cut off in the name of Jesus.

Shame and disgrace are of no kinship, but success and victory are my inheritance.

For I shall bear and produce, multiply and replenish, and subdue and dominate in Jesus' name.

Unmotivated

Father, give me the ability to manage my current situations and circumstances. Help me function even when dismay is seeking me out.

Give me strength and courage, for the race isn't given to the swift but to the one who endures.

As I continue to push, allow Your Spirit to lead me and victories to be along the journey.

For Your Word says, I will see greater and since You are truth, allow my mind, hands, and feet to move in accordance with your truth.

Trusting God

Lord, bless are those who take refuge in You. I shall rest in Your ability and willingness. When my mind is racing and doubt is roaming, I shall rest in thee. In knowing that you are a deliverer of Your people, I shall rest in thee. When Your words are few, but Your promises are many, l shall rest in thee. As You silence every voice and threat of the enemy, I shall rest in thee. As you set up a standard and contend on my behalf, I shall rest in thee. As you guide and direct, I shall rest in thee. As you send protective angels on assignment concerning me, I shall rest in thee.

New Territory

Father, as You provide new territory and Your Spirit to sends me out, allow seasons of lack and barrenness not to travel along.

I declare doors are opened wide and provision has gone ahead.

As my territory enlarges, allow my capacity to increase.

No weapon formed shall prosper, and ALL holes designed to disturb the surface shall be covered and filled.

Allow directive angels to assist me and protective angels to stand guard.

There shall be no demonic or evil trespassing in Jesus' name.

Fruitfulness

As I put my hands to work and my feet to move, I declare fruitfulness. As I remember to give you praise and admiration, release seeds of impact, encouragement, and strength. Father cause a return of increase, overflow, and gained ground. As the grounds yields, allow me the ability and access to gather. As your hand extends as a branch, I shall steward well over my increase. Resources are much, my hunger is satisfied, and my thirst is quenched in Jesus' name.

Overcoming Mistakes

I declare I will not ponder on mistakes and missed opportunities of the past, but will know that all things work together for my good, and as I trust in You, I am reminded that You are the One who changes times and seasons. This is my ear's time of hearing and listening, my heart's time of receiving and believing, my mind's time of perceiving and conceiving, and my mouth's time of speaking and decreeing. I am comforted in your redeeming ability and I shall put my trust in thee in Jesus' name.

Direction

Father, as You are aligning me, I will not create a maze where you have already set provision. I will look to the hill for help and set my thoughts above. I am free of false imagination, false burdens, wishing upon a star, roller coaster patterns, cycles of failure, and thoughts of delusion. I decree increase in my ability to cast down and bring all false hood into captivity in Jesus' name.

Control Over One's Emotions

I will not be up and down in my emotions. My emotions will not toss me around. They will not cause me to be distracted and frustrated. I align my thoughts to become that of Christ. I welcome both peace and joy. As I guard my ears, eyes, and heart gate, I contend not with flesh but fellowship with that of the spirit. As I seek stability, my knees will not buckle and my faith shall not fail in Jesus' name.

Enemy Pursuing

I declare my enemy will not take meat out of my mouth and food off of my table. Nothing shall be stalled, stolen, forfeited, destroyed, or murdered. Everything connected to me has breath, life, and abundance. Although the enemy desires to devour me and feast on my dry bones, he and his seed shall starve in their gluttony. The enemy has no place at my table and shall receive no portion of my now or next in Jesus' name.

Uncertainty

Father, for there is no uncertainty concerning You, so let not my perception and blinded understanding cause me to be wayward. Your promises are with assignment and I am a recipient. Your direction is with purpose and wrong thoughts are not invited along the way. I put them under my feet and silence their voice. Allow me to be wise and embrace growth along the way. Allow my sight to no longer dominate my faith and my failure to no longer dominate my hands in Jesus' name.

About the Author

Tim Vangure is a Degreed Life Coach, Mentor, Prayer Strategist, and Intercessor. With a Master's Degree in Human Services Counseling and over fifteen years in the areas of education, mental and behavioral health, Tim has a distinct passion for helping others. Tim believes it is important to not only support those you serve, but to cheer for them along the way.